Reviews of
Disrupting Philanthropy

"A **major achievement**. . . . I was amazed at the breadth and depth of the coverage and equally remarkable was the fact that the document is readable. . . . A **superb piece of work** that will surely help to move the revolution in positive directions."

> — William Dietel, Chairman, GuideStar International, and former President, Rockefeller Brothers Fund

"A **tour de force** on the impact of digital technology on philanthropy."

> —Sean Stannard-Stockton, *Tactical Philanthropy* blog

"A **fascinating read** for anyone interested in the future of the field of social entrepreneurship as it examines the recent growth and increased power of networking for good, and it highlights the huge opportunity ahead for addressing large-scale social challenges."

> —Tyler Spalding, Ashoka.org

"The **first robust assessment** of the philanthropy + technology intersection to come around in a long time."

> —Christine Egger, Co-Director, Social Actions

"[The authors have] in this paper not only mapped but also in a way legitimized the insurgent world of online philanthropy and emergent social-benefit networks. . . . [*Disrupting Philanthropy*] is **ideal to teach** from, and so gives 'gravitas' to what has to me felt like an almost recreational sideline, playing about on the net. It may turn out that such play has been the most serious work many of us have done."

> —Phil Cubeta, *Gift Hub* blog

DISRUPTING
PHILANTHROPY
Technology and the
Future of the Social Sector

DISRUPTING
PHILANTHROPY

Technology and the
Future of the Social Sector

LUCY BERNHOLZ
with EDWARD SKLOOT *and* BARRY VARELA

Center for Strategic Philanthropy and Civil Society
Sanford School of Public Policy
Duke University

Acknowledgments

The authors wish to thank the following individuals for their contributions to *Disrupting Philanthropy*: Diana Aviv, Akhtar Badshah, David Bollier, John Bracken, Sarah Burdick, Robin Ganzert, Will Heaton, Lakshmi Karan, Geoff Livingston, Darin McKeever, Jane Meseck, Mario Morino, Marcus Peacock, Susan Promislo, Lee Rainie, Kyle Reis, Patrick Sabol, Brad Smith, Melissa Stevens, and Debby Visser; and everyone who commented on the draft versions at Philanthropy 2173 and Philanthropy Central and through Twitter.

Duke
SANFORD
SCHOOL OF PUBLIC POLICY

Center for Strategic Philanthropy and Civil Society
Sanford School of Public Policy
Duke University
201 Science Drive
Durham, NC 27708

BLUEPRINT r+d
research + design for philanthropy

Blueprint Research & Design
720 Market Street, Suite 900
San Francisco, CA 94102

Book design by Randi Scherwin, Scherwin Design, LLC

ISBN 1453606947
Funding for *Disrupting Philanthropy* was provided by the John D. and Catherine T. MacArthur Foundation.

June 2010

Contents

Summary

This monograph explores the immediate and longer-term implications of networked digital technologies for philanthropy. Our claim is that information networks are transforming philanthropy. Enormous databases and powerful new visualization tools can be accessed instantly by anyone, at any time.

We provide a brief overview of the philanthropic landscape, followed by an explanation of the "long tail" of giving and receiving. Case studies of FasterCures and the Edna McConnell Clark Foundation show how information networks have transformed the grantmaking strategies of some institutional funders. Next, we examine how networked technologies are affecting five philanthropic practices:

- *Setting goals and formulating strategy*: how funders and enterprises make decisions about what to do, where, and how.

- *Building social capital*: how funders and enterprises support one another, cooperate, and collaborate.

- *Measuring progress*: how funders and enterprises set benchmarks, measure outputs, and make course corrections along the way.

- *Measuring outcomes and impact*: how funders and enterprises know whether what they've done has made a difference.

- *Accounting for the work*: how funders and enterprises account for what they do, to the public at large and to regulators.

We then offer a glimpse of what is to come. While the future is unknowable to a large degree, we feel confident in predicting we'll see an increase in the following three phenomena:

- New blendings of market-based and nonmarket solutions.

- Networked, boundaryless, and often temporary alliances that call for the creation of new ways of activating, coordinating, and governing cooperative efforts.

- More and better data, more readily available and at lower cost.

We conclude by pointing out that inequities of access and capacity prevent many individuals and institutions from benefitting from information networks. We believe the next decade will see explosive growth in networking for good, creating opportunities for creative solutions to large social problems.

Introduction

A decade ago, the landscape of philanthropy was relatively simple. There were foundations—private, community, and corporate—that awarded grants to nonprofits. Some of the larger staffed foundations also offered "technical assistance" to their grantees and undertook other activities such as convening meetings, engaging in advocacy, and financing litigation. Community foundations administered unrestricted, restricted, and donor-advised funds. Individuals gave money to nonprofits as well, mainly through personal checks or cash (while living) and bequests (upon death).

Ten years ago, givers both institutional and individual gathered information about nonprofits mainly through word-of-mouth. There was no easy way for foundation executives, let alone average citizens, to compare the financial health or budget-allocation practices of different organizations. Today, ratings services like Charity Navigator and Charity Guide assemble, analyze, and make available data on tens of thousands of organizations.

Ten years ago, commercial investment firms were small players on the philanthropic landscape. Today, companies like Charles Schwab and Fidelity Investments offer wide ranges of products for donors, including advised funds, foundation management services, and socially responsible investment vehicles.

Ten years ago, socially responsible investment was a niche concern mainly of universities, labor unions, and a few pension funds. Today, socially responsible investment accounts for more than 10% of professionally managed investment funds and is expected to total $3 trillion by next year.

Ten years ago, individual citizens were unable to contribute directly in response to a natural disaster like the 2001 Gujarat, India, earthquake. The best they could do was send money to a large international nonprofit like the American Red Cross. Today, a worldwide community of "crisis mappers," using satellite imagery and on-the-ground information reported via cell phone, helps coordinate responses to complex humanitarian emergencies.

Ten years ago, microfinance was entirely top-down—from large institutional lenders to small borrowers. Today, anyone can lend $25 to entrepreneurs located anywhere on the globe.

Information networks—the Internet primarily, and increasingly SMS (text-messaging) and 3G (smart-phone) cell phone technologies—are overturning core practices of philanthropic foundations and individuals. Enormous databases and powerful new visualization tools can be accessed instantly by anyone, at any time. A decade of experimentation in online giving, social enterprise, and collaboration has brought us to a place from which innovation around enterprise forms, governance, and finance will only accelerate.

The legal scholar Yochai Benkler has observed that the "networked information economy" that emerged over the past two decades is rooted in a "communications environment built on cheap processors with high computational capabilities, interconnected in a pervasive network" (i.e., the Internet) and is "centered on information (financial services, accounting, software, science) and cultural (films, music) production." The shift from a centralized, top-down, often impenetrable information economy to a networked information economy has allowed "nonmarket, nonproprietary motivations and organizational forms [to become] more important to the information production system." It has also enabled "the rise of effective, large-scale cooperative efforts—peer production of information, knowledge, and culture." [1]

As we scan the landscape of philanthropy, we'll see these themes—the importance of *nonmarket, nonproprietary motivations and organizational forms* and the emergence of *effective, large-scale cooperative efforts*—lurking constantly just below the surface.

The widespread availability of broadband Internet access and the near ubiquity of SMS and 3G cell phone networks give everyone the tools of both production and consumption. They expand individuals' sense of empowerment and lead to profound changes in expectations and norms. What information matters to funders and nonprofits? Who has it? Who owns it? How do we share it? How do we collaborate around common issues? How quickly can individuals and groups act when information is accessible 24/7?

In 1911, Andrew Carnegie created a general-purpose philanthropic entity—the foundation in its modern form. Two years later, John D. Rockefeller established the Rockefeller Foundation. Both men found that, to provide money and know-how in support of the social good, they needed to create centralized, vertically integrated institutions modeled on the big businesses (steel, oil) from which their fortunes derived. This institutional structure has remained the predominant model for organized philanthropy for almost a century. Today, peer-supported, data-informed, passion-activated, and technology-enabled networks represent a new structural form in philanthropy, and the institutions that support them will need to be as flexible, scalable, and portable as the networks they serve.

On the cusp of the first modern foundation's centennial, we may be looking at the dawn of a new form of organizing, giving, and governing that is better informed, more aware of complex systems, more collaborative, more personal, more nimble, and ultimately, perhaps, more effective.

---

[1] Benkler, Yochai, *The Wealth of Networks: How Social Production Transforms Markets and Freedom.* New Haven and London: Yale University Press, 206, pp. 3-4.

The Philanthropic Landscape

Philanthropy is the donation of money or labor toward the production of social good.[2] The vehicles through which Americans give include:

- Private foundations, ranging from small, unstaffed family foundations to large, professionally staffed multibillion-dollar institutions.

- Corporate foundations.

- Unrestricted, restricted, and donor-advised funds held by community foundations.

- Unrestricted, restricted, and donor-advised funds administered by religious, ethnic, or racial community groups such as the Jewish Federations.

- Donor-advised funds administered by commercial institutions such as Fidelity, Schwab, Vanguard, and National Philanthropic Trust.

- Donor-advised funds administered by freestanding institutions such as the American Endowment Foundation.

---

[2] In the American tradition (less so in the British), a distinction is drawn between *charity*, which seeks to alleviate immediate human suffering, and *philanthropy*, which seeks to solve or mitigate complex social problems that neither governments nor markets have been able, or seen fit, to fix. For the purposes of this monograph, "philanthropy" will be understood to include both impulses.

- Donor networks, such as the Global Impact Investing Network's Investors' Council and the Growth Philanthropy Network, socially responsible investment clubs, and similar organizations.

- Individual donations of money and labor.

- Bequests.

Many nonprofits build much of their operating and capital budgets through sales of products and/or fees for service, including from the government. Indeed, nonprofits cumulatively receive far more money from the public sector (local, state, and federal governments) than they do from the private sector (foundations and individuals).

Despite the prominence of very large foundations like the Bill & Melinda Gates Foundation, individual donations of money and labor are the largest component of philanthropy, annually constituting about 75% of the total.[3]

FOUNDATION FACTS AND FIGURES

Total U.S. giving in 2008 was estimated to be $307.65 billion. Of that total, about $45.6 billion was given by foundations.

There are about 75,000 private foundations, 2,500 corporate foundations, and 700 community foundations in the United States.

Of those foundations, about 28,000 have assets of less than $1 million; 47,000 have assets between $1 million and $10 million; 3,200 between $10 million and $25 million; and 2,700 have assets over $25 million.

In 2006, there were about 3,200 private and community foundations with paid staff. The total number of staff employed by foundations was about 17,500.

Figures come from the Foundation Center, the Urban Institute, the IRS, and other sources, and are presented here as rough estimates.

---

[3] GivingUSA Foundation, http://www.philanthropy.iupui.edu/News/2009/docs/GivingReaches300billion_06102009.pdf

Americans also contribute to the production of social good by investing in enterprises that purport to produce both financial and social returns—the "double bottom line." Because some potential income is, presumably, foregone by the decision to invest in companies that do good, some percentage of the estimated $2.71 trillion held in "socially responsible investment" funds[4] should be considered social good finance as well.

Furthermore, a range of entities assist, support, and facilitate giving. They are not themselves sources of money, but rather help steer where the money goes. They are frequently known as *intermediaries*; some are organized as nonprofits, others as profit-making. These entities include:

- Affinity groups of foundations organized around such rubrics as geography (Southeastern Council of Foundations), program area (Grantmakers in Film & Electronic Media), giving vehicle (PRI Makers Network), and profession (Grants Managers Network).

- Back-office support providers—attorneys, accountants, wealth managers, and the service professionals who assist donors, including family offices, and trust companies—and outsourced servicing firms for private foundations such as Foundation Source.

- Philanthropy advisors who counsel individuals and families and who help establish and manage family foundations.

- Commercial institutions that offer donor-advised funds and socially responsible investment options.

- Online philanthropy marketplaces. Sites such as GlobalGiving, DonorsChoose, and VolunteerMatch facilitate donations of money or labor. Other sites, such as Kiva, MyC4, and the Social Impact Exchange, facilitate loans and other forms of

---

[4] There is no single industry standard for defining or measuring socially responsible investment. See the discussion at http://philanthropy.blogspot.com/2009/09/impact-investing-index.html.

investment. Online information hubs such as GuideStar, GiveWell, and Charity Navigator describe and assess the quality of nonprofits.

The last category represents a genuinely new development in the philanthropic landscape. These sites can potentially connect a vast number of potential donors (institutional and individual) to a vast number of potential recipients. They service the so-called long tail.

Philanthropy's Long Tails

The *long tail* is a marketing strategy that connects products that have relatively small customer bases to those customers. Large companies such as Amazon and Netflix service the long tail by stocking not only very popular titles like the latest Dan Brown novel or Jim Carrey movie— products that may have millions of customers—but also thousands of things like poetry collections and documentaries: products that may have only a few hundred customers each. Cumulatively, the long tail of books sold by Amazon—ten copies of a scholarly study here, twenty copies of a memoir there—exceeds the sales of best-sellers.[5]

In the same way that Amazon allows the 200 individuals in the world who are interested in reading about some esoteric topic find the 10 books written on that topic, online philanthropy marketplaces allow individuals to find, evaluate, and invest in or fund the small enterprise or project that is of interest to them. And conversely, online marketplaces allow the small enterprise to find the few individuals willing to invest in or fund it. The long tail of philanthropy describes this dispersion of resources contributed for social good: millions of people, each providing small amounts of money to tens of thousands of enterprises.

Figure 1, "The Long Tail of Giving," shows how the funder market is organized. In 2008, the 400 largest foundation givers ranged from the Gates

[5] Brynjolffson, Smith, and Hu, in "Consumer Surplus in the Digital Economy: Estimating the Value of Increased Product Variety at Online Booksellers" (2003), calculated that about 48% of Amazon's book sales came from titles outside the top 40,000 sellers. Since "best-seller" is usually taken to mean only the top 100 sellers, it's safe to say that more than half of Amazon's sales come from non-best-sellers.

Foundation, which gave $2.8 billion, to the Greater St. Louis Community Foundation, which gave $14.4 million; cumulatively, the 400 gave $22.2 billion.[6] The 60 largest individual donors[7] ranged from the late Leona Helmsley, who left $5.2 billion to create a charitable foundation, to Oscar Tang, who gave $25 million to Phillips Andover Academy; cumulately, the 60 gave $10.6 billion. Together, the 400 foundations and 60 individuals gave about $32.8 billion to charitable causes in 2008—a small portion of the $307.7 billion given by all donors.

Online information exchanges focus on the long tail that makes up the right-hand side of Figure 1: the millions of smaller donors who, cumulatively, account for about eight times as many dollars as do the very biggest institutional and individual givers. It is the similarity between marketing on the long tail (poetry chapbooks v. best-sellers) and giving on the long tail (you and I, each with $200, v. the Gates Foundation) that is crucial to understanding one feature of the new philanthropic landscape.

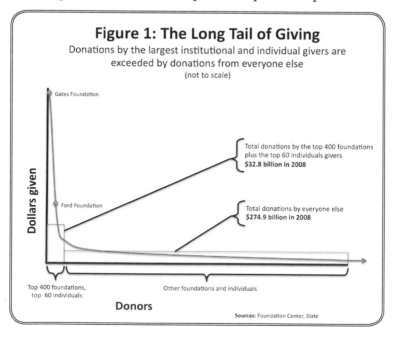

Figure 1: The Long Tail of Giving

Donations by the largest institutional and individual givers are exceeded by donations from everyone else
(not to scale)

Gates Foundation

Total donations by the top 400 foundations plus the top 60 individuals givers
$32.8 billion in 2008

Ford Foundation

Total donations by everyone else
$274.9 billion in 2008

Dollars given

Top 400 foundations, top 60 individuals

Other foundations and individuals

Donors

Sources: Foundation Center, *Slate*

---

[6] Figures drawn from the Foundation Center's Foundation Directory Online.

[7] *Slate*, "*Slate* 60: The Largest Charitable Contributions of 2008." Retreived from http://www.slate.com/id/2209500/workarea/3/.

Figure 2, "The Long Tail of Receiving," shows how the nonprofit market is organized. (Figures come from the National Center for Charitable Statistics and are based on the approximately 355,000 non-foundation nonprofits that filed tax returns in 2008.) As with the funder market, which is populated on the left-hand side by big foundations and high-net-worth individuals, large organizations such as the United Way, the Salvation Army, and major universities and medical centers make up the left-hand side of the recipient market. In contrast to the giving market, in which the big foundations and high-net-worth individuals do not outweigh the millions of small donors, the large nonprofits in the recipient market take in the lion's share of donations. In 2008, the approximately 40% of nonprofits with assets greater than $250,000 received almost 95% of donations. The over 200,000 nonprofits with assets less than $250,000 received only about 5% of donations. There is a long tail of receiving, but it's a starved tail.

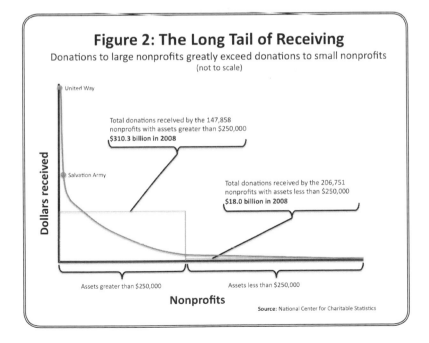

Figure 2: The Long Tail of Receiving
Donations to large nonprofits greatly exceed donations to small nonprofits
(not to scale)

Dollars received

United Way

Total donations received by the 147,858
nonprofits with assets greater than $250,000
$310.3 billion in 2008

Salvation Army

Total donations received by the 206,751
nonprofits with assets less than $250,000
$18.0 billion in 2008

Assets greater than $250,000   Assets less than $250,000

Nonprofits

Source: National Center for Charitable Statistics

Transactional philanthropy sites facilitate direct giving and lending by individuals to enterprises *without regard to geographical location*. The novelty of this arrangement can't be overstated. Ten years ago, the average American's philanthropic activity was limited to volunteering or donating to a local nonprofit (often a church or church-run operation like a soup kitchen), participating in a United Way fund drive, volunteering at the local chapter of one of the large civil-society organizations (Rotary, Habitat for Humanity, Boy Scouts of America), or writing a check to a prominent national or international nonprofit (American Cancer Society, World Wildlife Fund, Amnesty International). Today, individuals can lend money to small business owners in Tanzania, learn about the leanest, closest-to-the-ground nonprofits in Haiti, or buy art supplies for a fourth-grade teacher in a rural school half a continent away. While it's true that, in the case of the Haitian earthquake for example, most Americans donated to the American Red Cross rather than seeking out indigenous Haitian nonprofits, the trend is clear: With each passing year, more people learn about alternative candidates for their charitable dollars, in fuller and more revealing detail. In 2008, online giving surpassed $15 billion dollars (more than 5% of total giving),[8] and in 2009, while foundation giving fell by a record 8.4%,[9] online giving rose by 5%.[10]

While we typically focus on online giving and lending marketplaces for their financial transactional value, they have as a byproduct also created two large new information repositories that are invaluable resources for both donors and doers. The first repository contains information about entrepreneurs, organizations, and causes around the world or around the corner. Every project featured on one of these sites is its own data point about needs and opportunities. The second repository contains data about giving patterns.

[8] MacLaughlin, Steve, "Giving USA Report for 2008 and Online Fundraising Estimates." Connections blog, June 10, 2009. Retrieved from http://forums.blackbaud.com/blogs/connections/archive/2009/06/10/giving-usa-report-for-2008-and-online-fundraising-estimates.aspx.

[9] Foundation Center, *Foundation Growth and Estimates: Current Outlook: 2010 Edition*, p. 1. Retrieved from http://foundationcenter.org/gainknowledge/research/pdf/fgge10.pdf.

[10] Barton, Noelle, and Nicole Wallace, "Online Giving Continues to Grow but at a Slower Pace, Chronicle Survey Finds." *Chronicle of Philanthropy*, April 18, 2010. Retrieved from http://philanthropy.com/article/Online-Giving-Grows-but-at-a/65089/?sid=&utm_source=&utm_medium=en.

The networked information economy is now beginning to influence the left-hand side of the funder market as well. The professionals who run foundations, donor-advised funds, trusts, and other philanthropic institutions increasingly rely on electronic grant application and management systems, online reporting forms, and so on. Foundations are beginning to experiment with sharing with peer organizations these systems and the data they produce, creating collaborative databases that can be *remixed, re-sorted,* and *reconfigured.*

Different uses of data are at the core of the behavioral and expectation changes fostered by information networks. Our individual use of search engines is proof enough of this. For many of us, the ability to find instantaneously what we are looking for whether it's a restaurant, a news item, or the balance in our retirement accounts—has changed how we behave. We're now so used to immediate access to data from almost anywhere that we're more likely to take note of it when we can't find it than when we can. Think of the last time your browser was slow, your connection to Google lost, or you were out of cell phone range. The degree to which we're comfortable with and depend on information networks indicates the degree to which we will demand more from them. A brief example: It's no longer enough to be in an unfamiliar city and be able to find an Indian restaurant within five blocks; we also expect to be able to find user-generated reviews of it.

We see this same rise in expectations around online philanthropy. We now have sites such as Social Actions or All for Good that pull together and make available multiple donation or volunteer opportunities in a given locale or on a certain issue. We can barter for or donate goods simply by posting on FreeCycle or Craigslist. Smart-phone applications such The Extraordinaries and Catalista let us donate mental labor wherever we are and whenever we like.

The next frontier is the blending of donations with investments. Online giving markets that manage charitable donations are merging with investor-level exchanges that manage social investments. In some cases, such as the Denmark-based site MyC4, the user determines on a case-by-case basis whether she is making a gift, a loan, or a profit-seeking investment. Other sites, such as Kickstarter, which supports artistic and cultural projects, acknowledge that the funds they drive to projects can be classified as investments, gifts, loans, or any combination of the above—leaving the decision to the funder and recipient and broadening the options of both.

On the soon-to-launch NeXii, individual registered users will be able to manage portfolios of grants and investments, track them against financial and social indices, and compare their own performances against those of other investors. NeXii is designed to be useful to individual investors, commercial investors with social goals, and endowment managers seeking to track all of their grants and social investments in one place.

Sites like NeXii are built on software developed for financial markets and data derived from the social sector. It remains to be seen whether these sites will become popular enough to significantly reduce the amount of money that now goes into donor-advised funds administered by commercial banks and community foundations—and if so, whether those institutions will find a way to adapt to, or even adopt, online social-investment platforms.

While we cannot predict which of today's online marketplaces will be leading in transactions processed a decade from now, it's clear that the aggregated data from those transactions will themselves be a key source of information for and about the sector. They will then become the starting point for the next round of innovation.

Stories of Change

To date, individual donors—those millions who make up the long tail of giving—have benefitted the most from technological innovation, flocking to online transaction markets to donate and invest, organizing fundraisers and activist events through Twitter, communicating political and social messages through texting, and coordinating disaster response through cell phones. But some foundations have recently moved energetically to use technology to enhance or even alter the way they do business. Here are two examples.

FASTERCURES

Michael Milken's years of experience in funding prostate cancer research drove him to reconsider what kind of leverage an endowed foundation could have in funding medical disease research. He came to believe that medical research was conducted inefficiently, even counterproductively, and that funders were part of the problem. He chose to focus his funding on strategies that could translate basic research into medical therapies and recognized the potential to amplify the impact of his own funding by drawing in others. With the launch of FasterCures and the FasterCures Philanthropy Advisory Service, Milken expanded this strategy to other diseases and disease research projects.[11]

---

[11] For example, Alzheimer's disease, malaria, multiple sclerosis, and tuberculosis.

At the heart of these efforts are changes to the way research institutions develop and share knowledge and how funders do the same.

FasterCures performs high-quality, independent research on a variety of diseases and disease research institutions. The research is made available on the web through its Philanthropy Advisory Service (PAS) information marketplace. PAS members increase their knowledge and understanding by accessing disease reports, organization reports, and searchable disease research project databases. The PAS marketplace increases funder efficiency by steering donations toward research on those diseases that appear to be closest to breakthrough and toward those institutions that score highest on assessment reports. It improves entire disease research fields by motivating institutions that receive poor assessments to improve their practices. And it eliminates the need for each PAS member to separately perform due diligence on multiple potential grantees, thereby solving one of the "reinventing the wheel" problems that continually plague organized philanthropy.

FasterCures is also changing how disease research organizations function, as they can now benchmark themselves against a set of independently generated and tracked standards, report their results against consistent parameters, and organize their work in new ways. FasterCures brings together disease research organizations to share ideas on knowledge development, organizational practices, community engagement, and research—so that if experts working in one disease arena have a breakthrough, the process of others' learning from the breakthrough and applying it can be accelerated. FasterCures has fostered a network of "cure entrepreneurs" to move innovative solutions across formerly siloed institutions and disease communities, and has invested heavily in building a data-based system for sharing funding research and strategies with donors and other foundations.

FasterCures is one example of a foundation-led effort to transform how both donors and doers work. It's built on the premise that donors will value in-depth analysis of a field and of the organizations engaged in it; and that competition, made possible by a networked information marketplace, can improve efficiency in whole fields. The FasterCures model may well prove to be effective for philanthropic work in almost any domain.

THE EDNA McCONNELL CLARK FOUNDATION

Similar outcomes, from a very different base, can be seen in the work of the Edna McConnell Clark Foundation (EMCF). Prior to the late 1990s, EMCF funded programs in five unconnected fields. When foundation president Michael Bailin challenged his board to increase impact by focusing its grantmaking in only one area, the board selected disadvantaged youth. Under Bailin and, since 2005, Nancy Roob, EMCF performed deep due diligence on and stringent evaluation of grantees, using what it learned to improve its own work over time and focus its strategy on "large, long-term investments in nonprofit organizations whose programs have been proven to produce positive outcomes and that have the potential for growth." Still, successful as the new approach was, it was not enough to achieve the foundation's mission of maximizing impact. In order to bring significant change to the lives of as many children as possible, EMCF concluded that it had to change the way other, similarly focused foundations worked as well.

EMCF began to pull together its several-year effort to collect, analyze, and use information about effective organizations in ways that would allow it to attract tens of millions of other philanthropic dollars to the work it was doing. This initiative, which EMCF calls the Growth Capital Aggregation Pilot (GCAP), positioned the foundation as the lead investor (committing $39 million) in a $120 million, multiyear fund to support, improve, and expand three sizable and effective social sector organizations: Nurse Family Partnership, Youth Villages, and Citizen Schools. By 2009, 22 other investors had committed the remaining $81 million, and the federal government had selected all three of the portfolio organizations as exemplary organizations worthy of public investment.

GCAP funders work from common metrics and coordinate payment schedules, and all organizations and the funders share financial models and outcomes. Using data as a centerpiece, EMCF led the development of a new kind of investment syndicate that has substantially expanded the reach of its partner organizations and helped improve the lives of tens of thousands of young people and their families. It has also taken the concept of funder collaboration to a new level and brought into the field tens of millions of dollars that otherwise might never have been forthcoming.

Five Philanthropic Practices

The stories of FasterCures and the Edna McConnell Clark Foundation reveal the fundamental shift that can take place in foundations when they use networks as a resource, sharing what they know and working with others to achieve a common goal. The stories illustrate five common philanthropic practices that have been reconceived and redeployed through technology- and data-driven innovation. They are:

- *Setting goals and formulating strategy*: how funders and enterprises make decisions about what to do, where, and how.

- *Building social capital*: how funders and enterprises support one another, cooperate, and collaborate.

- *Measuring progress*: how funders and enterprises set benchmarks, measure outputs, and make course corrections along the way.

- *Measuring outcomes and impact*: how funders and enterprises know whether what they've done has made a difference.

- *Accounting for the work*: how funders and enterprises account for what they do, to the public at large and to regulators.

The stories that follow highlight examples of donors and organizations adopting or experimenting with various technological tools in each of the above practice areas. For simplicity's sake, we refer simply to funders (including individuals and institutions) and enterprises (including nonprofits, intermediaries, and for-profit social-purposed companies), keeping in mind that both of these categories are quite diverse.

SETTING GOALS AND FORMULATING STRATEGY
How Funders and Enterprises Make Decisions About What to Do, Where, and How

How do funders decide what social problem to tackle? How do they choose what to fund? Often the answer to both of these questions is tied to personal passion and area of expertise, but there is an increasingly visible use of information assessment and market research to inform these choices.

Online philanthropy marketplaces allow individuals to do the kind of enterprise assessment that previously only staffed foundations (and not many of those) could afford to do. They allow potential donors to sift and sort by geography, gender, social issue, funding need, and other variables before deciding on where to direct their gifts. For example, a user interested in water-quality issues might choose between lending to a farmer to invest in a water pump, donating to a nonprofit water pump manufacturer, making a small investment in a new water cleaning technology, or supporting a community fighting to retain control of its local water supply. Whereas finding these options in the past might have taken years of research and access to local experts in several countries—actions that, in many cases, are still indispensable—better, clearer choices can now be made by anyone with access to an Internet connection.

For larger institutional funders, the tools for assessing a field have also changed. Their process often begins at the strategy-setting stage, where they might commission an analysis of funding patterns and then map that information against public data on needs or demographics. Tools such as Gap minder—a data visualization tool that makes relationships between data sets easy to see—are now readily available. Network analysis, which can help identify and depict patterns of relationships among individuals, organizations, or funders, is another increasingly useful means of understanding a situation.[12]

The availability of such useful, precise, and comparable information can enable funders to envision strategies, time frames, and partnerships that were unimaginable a decade ago. The new tools have also led more funders to require "evidence-based" proposals.

Foundation professionals and social investors are slowly beginning to seek external input into their strategy-formation practices. For example, the Lumina Foundation for Education has posted its strategic planning process, the plan itself, and the progress measures being used on an interactive website to which the public can contribute comments. The foundation also has a YouTube channel where the public can watch and comment on video interviews with key decision makers. The Peery Foundation in Palo Alto, California, recently pushed its strategic planning conversations into public view using Twitter—welcoming thoughts, sharing its planning tools, and actively discussing its ideas with anyone who followed the foundation's board or staff members. The Twitter discussions prompted prominent bloggers to weigh in on the process.

These experiments move us in the direction of using the web to crowdsource[13] strategies for giving. One well-known example comes from Paul Buchheit, an early Google employee, who wrote a blog post[14] looking for advice on his donor-advised fund and then built a series

---

[12] For example, in its Savings for Change initiative, Oxfam has used networks of participants to spread the impact of a specific project. See Holley, June, "The Viral Giving Network," *Network Weaving* blog, February 25, 2009. Retrieved from http://networkweaver.blogspot.com/2009/02/viral-giving-network.html.

[13] A term coined by the writer Jeff Howe in a 2006 article in *Wired* magazine to describe the phenomenon of using large, dispersed groups of amateurs networked through the web to do work that was previously performed by solitary experts or units within larger institutions. See Howe, Jeff, "The Rise of Crowdsourcing." *Wired*, June 2006. Retrieved from http://www.wired.com/wired/archive/14.06/crowds.html.

[14] Buchheit, Paul, "Collaborative Charity." *Paul Buchheit* blog, June 25, 2009. Retrieved from http://paulbuchheit.blogspot.com/2009/06/collaborative-charity.html.

of online tools—including a Google moderated voting site[15] and a FriendFeed Group—enabling anyone to post suggestions. The British Government proposed a similar project to guide some of its funding for international aid.[16] The John S. and James L. Knight Foundation has used crowdsourcing tactics in its News Challenge grants program, and in 2007, the David and Lucile Packard Foundation used a wiki[17] to solicit possible approaches to dealing with the problem of nitrogen pollution. By availing themselves of information networks, these grant makers increased the variety of expertise and widened the range of perspectives that shaped their philanthropic strategies.

Another crowd-based strategy, the incentivizing prize[18] competition[19] is structured to generate a solution to a specified social or technical problems rather than to reward laudable accomplishment in retrospect. X Prize Foundation competitions leverage philanthropic investment by inducing participants to spend more money cumulatively than is offered as a prize. The prize challenges extended by the Rockefeller Foundation and administered by InnoCentive draw upon the talents and expertise of individuals who might not otherwise devote their time and energy to solving problems in the social sphere. More conventional prizes, awarded on the basis of merit, include ASHOKA's Changemakers, the MacArthur Foundation's Digital Media and Learning Competition, and the Case Foundation's "Change Begins with Me" challenge. All engage new types of partners in both discussing issues and developing solutions.

[15] Google Moderator, "Collaborative Charity." Retrieved from http://www.google.com/moderator/#15/e=1fa8&t=1fa8.40&f=1fa8.d8b0.

[16] Savage, Michael, "Let Voters Decide Aid Projects, Say Tories." *The Independent* (U.K.), July 13, 2009. Retrieved from http://www.independent.co.uk/news/uk/politics/let-voters-decide-aid-projects-say-tories-1743360.html.

[17] Spitfire Strategies, *Analysis of a Nitrogen Wiki: The David and Lucile Packard Foundation's Experiment with Online Collaboration.* Retrieved from http://www.packard.org/assets/files/capacity%20building%20and%20phil/organizational%20effectiveness/phil%20networks%20exploration/nitrogen_wiki_report_110507_FINAL.pdf.

[18] Leerberg, Matthew, "Incentivizing Prizes: How Foundations Can Utilize Prizes to Generate Solution to the Most Intractable Social Problems." Paper written for Professor Joel Fleishman's Public Policy Studies 280 class, "The Idea of the Voluntary Society: Philanthropy, the Not-for-profit Sector, and Public Policy," 2006. Interim working paper, subject to revision. Retrieved from http://cspcs.sanford.duke.edu/sites/default/files/Leerberg-Incentivizing-Prizes.pdf.

[19] McKinsey & Company, *"And the Winner Is . . .": Capturing the Promise of Philanthropic Prizes.* McKinsey & Company, 2009. Retrieved from http://www.mckinsey.com/clientservice/Social_Sector/our_practices/Philanthropy/Knowledge_highlights/And_the_winner_is.aspx.

BUILDING SOCIAL CAPITAL
How Funders and Enterprises Support One Another, Cooperate, and Collaborate

Much of the recent excitement about technology has involved social networks—online communities where individuals and institutions can share information and interests, find friends and colleagues, and encourage one another to take action on issues or donate to causes. The names of some of these communities are familiar—Facebook, MySpace, LinkedIn, Twitter. However, the extent of their philanthropic impacts is unclear. A 2009 analysis in the *Washington Post*[20] of the funds raised through Facebook led to a high-spirited disagreement[21] on blogs,[22] as some argued that the tools were therefore useless while others focused on the networks as awareness-raisers, not fundraisers.

The ecology of social networks has diversified to include enterprises besides the large general-interest platforms like Facebook. For example, Ning is a web company that allows anyone to create a social network incorporating customized branding, visual design, and choice of features. Ning hosts more than 1,000 networks of nonprofit organizations, foundations, and charities. Similarly, BigTent Design supports networks specifically for community groups. Connecting to like-minded people, hearing from supporters, and sharing information are key goals for these enterprises. These same goals explain the use of other digital tools that facilitate outreach and engagement, including Twitter, blogs, and virtual worlds such as Second Life.

The establishment of cell phone networks in some of the remotest parts of the world, as well as the low cost of the phones themselves, has created opportunities for previously isolated individuals and communities to connect and collaborate in unprecedented ways. For example, FrontlineSMS, an open-source software program that

[20] Hart, Kim, and Megan Greenwell, "To Nonprofits Seeking Cash, Facebook App Isn't so Green." *Washington Post*, April 22, 2009. Retrieved from http://www.washingtonpost.com/wp-dyn/content/article/2009/04/21/AR2009042103786.html.culosis.

[21] Kanter, Beth, "Hello, Washington Post: Dollars Per Facebook Donor Is Not the Right Metric for Success." *Beth's Blog*, April 22, 2009. Retrieved from http://beth.typepad.com/beths_blog/2009/04/hello-washington-post-dolllars-per-facebook-donor-is-not-the-right-metric-for-success.html.

[22] MacLaughlin, Steve, "Creating a Social Networking Strategy." *Connections blog*, April 22, 2009. Retrieved from http://forums.blackbaud.com/blogs/connections/archive/2009/04/22/creating-a-social-networking-strategy-part-0.aspx.

enables mobile-phone users to send text messages to large groups, has been used by local individuals and enterprises to post updates on commodity market conditions in rural Peru, report the location of landmine victims in Cambodia, and record human rights violations in Ghana.

As well as cell phones, GPS and Internet-based mapping programs have reduced the isolation that remote, often poor communities have struggled with. Ushahidi began in 2008 as a simple platform for incorporating field reports of political violence in Kenya into Google Maps. By fall 2009, the Ushahidi platform had been used to monitor national elections in India and Mexico and track medical-supply shortages in Malawi and Zambia. Ushahidi isn't for just the geographically remote; in January 2010, an Ushahidi offshoot helped coordinate storm cleanup after Washington, D.C.'s "Snowmaggedon."

In the months since a major earthquake devastated Haiti, we have seen how quickly and on how large a scale individuals and organizations can collaborate on behalf of others. In a matter of days, three platforms—text donations, Twitter, and Facebook—moved from the philanthropic margins to the center of both fundraising and volunteer activity. A series of loosely managed, globally dispersed weekend CrisisCamps took place on several continents over many weeks. Volunteers at these events produced dozens of software tools to help relief workers on the ground and in government agencies. Basing its work on the Ushahidi platform and launched in October 2009, the International Network of Crisis Mappers (CM*Net) responded to the Haiti earthquake by rapidly gathering and disseminating information on the location of, among other things, safe water resources, disease outbreaks, fuel sources, and hospitals and medical aid stations. CM*Net-produced data were used by the U.S. military, the Haitian government, and dozens of nonprofits in planning and coordinating their response. Networked citizens contributed an unprecedented amount of private money and expertise in a remarkably short period of time. Many used social networks to spread word of the disaster, round up funds and volunteers, and stay informed over time about developments in Port-au-Prince. To date, more than $1 billion has been collected for relief and reconstruction, with the average donation via the Internet at a mere $10. A vast, previously untapped population of contributors was reached through ubiquitous information networks. When brought together around a single crisis, smaller groups and individuals can now play a decidedly important role in finding and implementing solutions.

A similar change is occurring in the ecology of conferences. Networking technologies encourage new kinds of collaboration at conferences organized around topics of interest to the social sector. Whereas these events used to be predicated on the idea that only those who'd paid registration fees and traveled long distances would be privy to what was discussed, many conference organizers now assume that the conversation will extend beyond the ballroom walls. For example, a 2009 conference on social capital markets[23] devoted several weeks before the event to building up awareness on blogs and Twitter, had volunteers updating Facebook and Flickr pages before, during, and after the event, showcased two different video channels, one live and one recorded,

{ CM*Net responded to the Haiti earthquake by rapidly gathering and disseminating information on the location of, among other things, safe water resources, disease outbreaks, fuel sources, and hospitals. } and equipped several participants with small video cameras to capture sessions as they happened. All of this information was posted online for the benefit of both those at the venue and those who could not attend. This commitment to making visible, and thus learnable, what was once literally held behind closed doors marks a major shift in our expectations about information and networks—and about conferences. Similar social media strategies are becoming *de rigueur* for major industry conclaves.

If funders want to support networked change agents, they may themselves have to adjust their expectations about what constitutes a legitimate, fund-worthy organization. Ushahidi, for example, was

---

[23] SoCap09. See http://www.socialcapitalmarkets.net/.

started by an unincorporated group of colleagues spread over two continents and several countries. Even though the informal, networked structure proved capable of building an effective platform for the advancement of social good, that same structure proved to be a stumbling block to raising foundation funds. It didn't conform to the organizational model funders understood and were comfortable with. We will see more such disconnects as enterprises that are "native to the digital world" continue to proliferate.[24]

MEASURING PROGRESS
How Funders and Enterprises Set Benchmarks, Measure Outputs, and Make Course Corrections Along the Way

Enterprises have led the way in seeking measures of progress that help them improve their work and fund-raise in a highly competitive grantmaking system. Facilitated by low-cost digital technology such as identity card readers that enable better tracking of service use, the ability to track inputs and outputs has grown more robust. With better tracking has come improved ability to analyze, share, and jointly produce measures and tracking systems of value. These improvements have, in turn, begun to alter the approach to, and value of, evaluation and assessment. Evaluation and assessment reports are still too often retrospective and anecdotal, and they still are not widely shared. But the culture of philanthropy is changing, and expectations surrounding evaluation and assessment are changing too.

Donors and investors are also actively engaged in developing whole new systems for measuring progress. Acumen Fund, an independent social investment fund focused on alleviating poverty in Asia and Africa, has begun developing internal measures of progress that can be used across its portfolios. Each portfolio addresses a distinct domain, such as job creation, health outcomes, or access to clean water. As Acumen progressed in this work, major partners such as Google and Salesforce.com joined in and began the push to create measures

---

[24] See the discussion at Bernholz, Lucy, "Change Native to the Digital World." Philanthropy 2173, June 16, 2009. Retrieved from http://philanthropy.blogspot.com/2009/06/change-native-to-digital-world.html.

and tracking systems that could be used by other organizations, as well as to enable it to raise more investment dollars. Doing so required the development of a shared taxonomy of outcomes and of systems that could track information within a single organization as well as feed into a common database. Thus was born the Pulse platform—a software system for tracking outcome measures. The Impact Reporting and Investing Standards (IRIS), a shared taxonomy of outcome definitions,[25] is currently being launched alongside the Pulse platform.

Another example of shared measures comes from the community development field. NeighborWorks America is a congressionally chartered nonprofit founded in 1978 to support community revitalization efforts around the country. About a decade ago, a group of community development leaders began to see the need for a measurement system that would go beyond capturing performance or outputs data such as houses built or jobs created to evaluating impact. An innovator in participatory (as opposed to third-party) outcomes evaluation, Success Measures offers a variety of web-based evaluation framework designs based on collaboratively developed and tested data collection tools and outcome indicators. Groups can aggregate data, download them to Excel to create spreadsheets and graphs, and contribute to the further refinement of Success Measures frameworks, tools, and indicators by sharing what they learned. To date more than 300 community development practitioners, intermediaries, funders, researchers, and evaluators have participated in the development of Success Measures.

Sharing progress reports and evaluations is one significant change; deriving them from actual participants is another, more complicated and costly one. One of the barriers in all measurement endeavors is the cost of reaching out to relevant constituents. Cutting corners by measuring proxy indicators may obscure, rather than clarify, what really happened to those affected by a given program. Networked technology can reduce the expense of obtaining on-the-ground data. Recently

---

[25] See the discussion at Global Impact Investing Network, "Impact Reporting and Investment Standards." Retrieved from http://www.globalimpactinvestingnetwork.org/cgi-bin/iowa/reporting/index.html,%20http:/venturebeat.com/2009/08/29/analytics-for-toeing-the-fine-lines-in-social-venture-investing/.

GlobalGiving, an online marketplace for donors around the world, watched as one local group sought comments via text messages on the impact of its work. Working in a small African village, the group's leaders handed out bumper stickers that asked people to text their thoughts about the program to a certain number. Anyone with an opinion could respond, anonymously, about the impact, management, and role of the organization in the community. The cost to gather the data? The cost of the bumper stickers. More sophisticated data collection and analysis of stakeholders is also underway, including efforts modeled on customer feedback and constituency voice. Keystone Accountability, a U.K.-based research and consulting firm, now offers a free tool on its website to enable nonprofit organizations to acquire anonymous constituent feedback.

Another example of how data can be collected in the era of social media can be found in the YouthTruth evaluation. A partnership between the Bill & Melinda Gates Foundation and the Center for Effective Philanthropy, YouthTruth distributed a survey (online, on social networks MySpace and Facebook, via email, and with the help of MTV) to high school students attending schools receiving funding from the Gates Foundation. The data collected are used to inform the schools, the funders, and the evaluators. Recognition of the value of the end-user experience is inherent in the process. Students have access to the information as well as other resources that might help them improve their schools. This type of evaluation turns subjects into actors. It changes dynamics at every level—when information is collected, from whom, how it's used, and who can analyze it—at a cost that is negligible when compared to traditional approaches.

Another approach, similar to FasterCures, is the creation of shared databases of organizations or projects. Examples include the Pennsylvania Cultural Database, Grantmakers for Film and Electronic Media's media database, and the newly launched Social Entrepreneur API. The issues covered range from cultural programming to non-U.S.-based nonprofit equivalent organizations, but the underlying practice and philosophy of these projects is the same—organize and make accessible data to make change easier, faster, and more catalytic.

These examples are only a few of many tools for measuring progress that now exist. A 2009 study by McKinsey & Company found more than 150 such tools being used in the American social sector. That study informed the creation of a database of these tools known as TRASI (which can be accessed for free, commented on, and improved) that is now housed at the Foundation Center.[26] Similarly, a recent analysis of shared metrics by FSG-Social Impact Advisors[27] provides several stories like the NeighborWorks example. That study is now hosted on a website[28] that invites readers to contribute additional examples and comment on those provided. In short, the very act of researching these issues has changed. It no longer suffices to document an issue and provide a snapshot in time. Many major studies now have companion websites that incorporate interactive conversations about the research and new resources as they are identified. These tools represent only the first steps in an ongoing process of improvement.

MEASURING OUTCOMES AND IMPACT
How Funders and Enterprises Know Whether What They've Done Has Made a Difference

The last decade has seen tremendous innovation around measuring social change. With roots that trace to both the United Way and public agency efforts at outcome reporting, the social sector has been hard at work trying to isolate, calculate, track, and report meaningful measures of impact. For several reasons, the pace of innovation in the last few years has accelerated.

First, singular efforts at calculating impact, such as the social return on investment (SROI) work begun at REDF (formerly called the Roberts Economic Development Fund) in the 1990s, have gradually gathered attention and respect, and given birth to numerous spin-off approaches.

[26] Foundation Center, "TRASI: Tools and Research for Assessing Social Impact." Retrieved from http://foundationcenter.org/trasi/.

[27] Kramer, Mark, Marcie Parkhurst, and Lalitha Vaidyanathan, *Breakthroughs in Shared Measurement and Social Impact.* FSG Social Impact Advisors, 2009. Retrieved from http://www.fsg-impact.org/ideas/item/breakthroughs_in_measurement.html.

[28] http://sharedmeasurementapproaches.pbworks.com/.

Second, a growing movement of social investment vehicles, run by people who want to develop data to improve the work, from program-related investments to social investment funds, has increased the pressure for quantifiable, comparable measures of social change.

Finally, the maturation of independent philanthropy advisory firms has required points of differentiation, and offering new ways to measure impact was one area of competitive advantage. This pressure to measure extends directly to the use of technology itself—the rapid rise of social media is paralleled by dynamic debates and rapid innovation in ways to measure the impact of these tools.[29]

The importance of measuring outcomes and impact has lately become the mantra of most large donors and investors. Some of the push has come from a new breed of funders who honed their skills (and earned their millions) in venture capital and investment banking. The recent financial collapse put more pressure on funders, who were forced to engage in a kind of triage on their existing grantees, to determine the quality of the grantee outcomes. The trend toward more and better measurement appears to be unstoppable—especially since we now have the tools to undertake it.

ACCOUNTING FOR THE WORK
How Funders and Enterprises Account for What They Do, to the Public and to Regulators

While measures of impact are important, there is yet a larger issue of accountability that these measures don't reach. That question has to do with the degree to which organizations in the social sector, both funders and enterprises, are held to account for their work to the broader public and to regulatory and tax agencies. At the most basic level, in the United States, this accountability is required, though hardly enforced, as part of the tax-exempt status afforded many of these organizations. Information networks are raising new questions: to whom is philanthropy accountable, and what is it accountable for?

[29] See the work of Chris Brogan, Beth Kanter, and K.D. Paine, among others.

Regulatory accountability for philanthropies in the U.S. is generally limited to financial issues—funds must be properly invested, tracked, paid out, and reported on. Both state and federal agencies require such reports, and much of the aggregate data that we have on the sector comes from analysis of the tax forms filed by nonprofit organizations, philanthropic foundations, and individual donors.

Some foundations are trying to establish subsector-wide norms and benchmarking tools. For example, the Community Foundation Insights toolkit is designed to help community foundations measure their costs, adjust their fees, and evaluate their staffing patterns. What once might have been shared only among a few colleagues personally acquainted with one another can now be captured for the field as a whole.[30] The Center for Effective Philanthropy's data sets on foundation responsiveness, grantee satisfaction, and board practices are another example of technology-enabled, industry-wide benchmarks. Some foundations, such as the William and Flora Hewlett, Geraldine R. Dodge, Surdna, and John A. Hartford, have posted their CEP reports on their websites. Many other foundations have used the feedback to change their policies and practices.

Grantsfire, an open platform that allows grants data to be aggregated, has just become a project of the Foundation Center, the sector's preeminent data source. In April 2010, GuideStar International and TechSoup Global announced a merger. The new enterprise is positioned to launch a global aggregator and repository of information on nonprofits—a single, searchable source for information on organizations everywhere.

Who ultimately *owns* social sector data is an unresolved issue for donors and enterprises. Voluntary efforts such as the Public Library of Science (PLoS) and Science Commons have laid the groundwork for sharing information in pursuit of common goals. In the public sector, research funded by the National Institutes of Health must be

---

[30] Another relevant example is the wiki of technology use by foundations, assembled by Blueprint Research & Design and now hosted at Northern California Grantmakers. See http://blueprintrd.pbworks.com/.

published in the openly accessible PubMed database within 12 months of work completion. In the case of philanthropy, because donors receive tax benefits—essentially, unrestricted grants from the government—foundations are quasi-public institutions. Data held by foundations would therefore seem to belong to the public.

Most foundations don't behave as if they, or the data they produce, are owned by the public. While a few funders have become more open by publishing grants applications on their websites, information about selection and performance rarely sees the light of day. The work of the Milken Foundation, FasterCures, and a few other philanthropies points the way toward a future of greater access to important information for the public good.

Glimpses of the Future

The technology expert Clay Shirky has observed, "Communications tools don't get socially interesting until they get technologically boring."[31] This is certainly the case in philanthropy. Philanthropy is, by its very nature, idiosyncratic and fragmented. A technology or practice must be widely adopted, and broadly transformative of individuals' expectations, before we can expect to see it make a real impact across philanthropic enterprises. Email; online shopping, banking, and bill paying; search engines; social networks; wikis; blogs; streaming music and video; newspaper and magazine online publication; GPS and online maps; cell phones; digital cameras—these are among the technological innovations that, to date, have changed people's behaviors, and most people now view them as "technologically boring." (Remember how amazing GPS was the first time you saw it? That was probably less than ten years ago. Now—yawn.)

As we have seen, networked information has already affected, in some domains, the way philanthropy is conducted and the way social good is produced. But philanthropy is not like the music or newspaper industries, which have been utterly transformed—mostly against the will of those who run record labels and newspapers—by information

---

[31] Shirky, Clay, *Here Comes Everybody: The Power of Organizing without Organizations.* London: Penguin Press, 2008, p. 105.

networks. While no record label can operate the same way it did ten years ago, and no newspaper can ignore the Internet, there are thousands of private foundations, and millions of individual donors, who disburse their charitable assets, whether money, time, expertise, or physical labor, using no technology that didn't exist in 1989 (or 1889, for that matter). Nevertheless, change is inevitable, and the further penetration of networked technologies into everyday life, among all social strata in all parts of the globe, would seem likewise to be inevitable.

Some of the changes that networked technologies will bring may not just fail to live up to expectations, but may also bring negative consequences. For example, the establishment of network-driven standardized metrics may direct resources toward easily measurable, low-cost, low-effect interventions at the expense of less easily quantifiable, but perhaps ultimately more important, activities. Similarly, while increased transparency is an important goal in philanthropy, there may be a point at which transparency limits creativity and risk taking. And there is no agreement in the funding world on what transparency means anyway.

Some technologies—virtual worlds, gaming—play only marginal roles in philanthropy at present. They have not yet induced widespread interest, let alone change. But as today's new technologies become commonplace, the next order of change—in behaviors and in expectations—will set in, and that is where we will see the early indications of what the future will hold. Here are three phenomena we expect to see more of in the future:

- New blendings of market-based and nonmarket solutions.

- Networked, boundaryless, and often temporary alliances that call for the creation of new ways of activating, coordinating, and governing cooperative efforts.

- More and better data, more readily available and at lower cost.

NEW BLENDINGS OF MARKET-BASED AND NONMARKET SOLUTIONS

Today, socially minded entrepreneurs don't have to choose *either* the market *or* the nonprofit sector. The ethic of the networked information economy—reinforced every time you use your Firefox browser to look up something on Wikipedia or watch a user-generated video on YouTube—states that people aren't motivated by profit alone, and that enterprise can generate *both* profit *and* social good.

We observe two seemingly contradictory impulses that, on reflection, may not be so contradictory. On the one hand, we see a proliferation of phenomena that harness market mechanisms to solve social problems: socially responsible investing, information marketplaces such as the FasterCures Philanthropy Advisory Service, B Corporations, low-profit limited liability companies (L3Cs).[32] On the other hand, we see an enormous commitment of time, energy, ingenuity, and know-how to nonmarket, nonproprietary phenomena that are themselves social goods: open-source software, wikis, Project Gutenberg. The blended value proposition developed by author and consultant Jed Emerson states "that all organizations, whether for-profit or not, create value that consists of economic, social and environmental value components—and that investors (whether market-rate, charitable or some mix of the two) simultaneously generate all three forms of value through providing capital to organizations."[33] We may be approaching a moment when the idea of blended value, which resolves the contradiction between market and nonmarket impulses, may become as commonplace as belief in the "invisible hand" of the market is today.

Over the past few decades, corporations have pushed for ever-longer periods of copyright protection and ever-broader interpretations of what can be copyrighted. In response, the foundation-supported nonprofit Creative Commons has established a "copyleft" licensing regime that accomplishes the inverse of what copyrights usually do: rather than restricting rights, Creative Commons licenses bestow them,

---

[32] For a pithy explanation of the L3C, see Takagi, Gene, "L3C—Low-profit Limited Liability Company." *Nonprofit Law* Blog, July 22, 2008. Retrieved from http://www.nonprofitlawblog.com/home/2008/07/l3c.html.

[33] Emerson, Jed, "What Is Blended Value?" BlendedValue.org, 2006-2010. Retrieved from http://www.blendedvalue.org/.

ensuring that a work placed in the public domain by its creator, as well as all works derivative of that work, remains there. In addition to texts and images, Creative Commons licenses cover scientific data, music, and video, and they are valid in countries all over the world. A 2009 study performed by the Berkman Center at Harvard Law School found that while "Open licenses promise significant value for foundations and for the public good and often for grantees as well," they are rarely used in the philanthropic sector, as "many grantees and foundations are relatively uninformed and inexperienced with open licenses."[34]

For many tasks, nonmarket entities and the self-organizing commons can compete with, and even outperform, the market because market players tend to have higher overhead costs in the form of advertising, talent recruitment, capital equipment, attorney fees, and so on. Funders can apply tremendous leverage by making relatively small investments in maintaining the infrastructure and information resources that enable nonmarket players to exist and flourish.[35]

NETWORKED, BOUNDARYLESS, AND OFTEN TEMPORARY ALLIANCES THAT CALL FOR THE CREATION OF NEW WAYS OF ACTIVATING, COORDINATING, AND GOVERNING COOPERATIVE EFFORTS

The transition from a relatively simple social economy to a complex social economy made up of a spectrum of financing sources and enterprise types has already begun.

On the funder side, we've seen a decade of experimentation with different kinds of peer networks. Just as an environmental program officer in a large foundation has a peer group of program officers at other foundations, environmentally focused individual donors are now connecting directly with their peers. The same thing is happening with regionally focused donors, activists interested in public data access, individuals who share the immigrant's diaspora experience, and those committed to global giving. Acumen Fund and the Edna McConnell

[34] Malone, Phil, "An Evaluation of Private Foundation Copyright Licensing Policies, Practices and Opportunities." Berkman Center for Internet & Society, Harvard University, 2009, pp. 46, 41. Retrieved from http://cyber.law.harvard.edu/sites/cyber.law.harvard.edu/files/OCL_for_Foundations_REPORT.pdf.

[35] The authors wish to thank David Bollier for elucidating this point about nonmarket efficiency and funder leverage.

Clark Foundation show how a data-driven portfolio approach can be used to attract donors to new forms of investing. Giving circles and Social Venture Partner communities bring together individuals who want to increase their philanthropic impact by working together. The Global Impact Investing Network's Investors' Council, SeaChange Capital Partners, the Nonprofit Finance Fund, and the Growth Philanthropy Network are all examples of new networks for donors and social investors.

We can expect that more and better networked information will lead to more and better collaborations and partnerships. Donors and doers will no longer be able to say that data are unavailable, or that they are too expensive to collect, in order to avoid working together. Donors and doers who do insist on going it alone may find themselves at a disadvantage when faced with networks of mutually supportive organizations and individuals.

Staffing foundations individually, especially small foundations, may cease to make sense. Consortia of active donors may begin to thrive, especially for place-based or thematic endeavors, boosting the case for donor engagement in philanthropy.

On the enterprise side, we see market-based enterprises such as B Corporations and L3Cs. As this monograph goes to press, there are 285 registered B Corps, including companies such as CleanFish, which works to preserve ocean biodiversity by changing the fishing industry, and Better World Books, an online book reseller that donates proceeds to literacy programs. B Corps also include retail outlets that function as employment development programs, such as Juma Ventures and Greyston Bakery. L3Cs include small, socially oriented enterprises such as Maine's Own Organic Milk (MOOMilk) and the Champlain Housing Loan Fund.

Network-enabled volunteer groups like Ushahidi are radically different from incorporated enterprises with bylaws, mission statements, formal boards of directors, and geographical limits. They operate outside the existing regulations for grant funding that require nonprofit organizational status. They are managed by individuals who seek social solutions, not monetary gain or market success, and they rely on new models of accountability. Led by volunteers and managed remotely with free software, Nonprofitmapping.org rates the states on the quality of data on nonprofits they make available, with the aim of improving state reporting standards. It's an example of how a virtual team, without an organizational home, permanent institutional affiliation, or shared locale, can work together to solve a big problem.

Similarly, volunteer-driven efforts that are, by design, here today and gone tomorrow—"flash" causes—can create tremendous impact by drawing attention to an issue. Some can even move a fair amount of money. In February 2009, charity: water raised hundreds of thousands of dollars through parties in more than 100 cities, all organized by volunteers via Twitter.[36] These dispersed, crowd-organized events are common tools of community organizing and political fundraising[37] and are increasingly present in campaigns for charitable support.

New organizational models will require new modes of governance. Most of the successful examples we can find of distributed governance, such as the ongoing development of the open-source software platform Linux, are made possible by norms and licenses that are unique to the software arena. For other kinds of ventures—such as in higher education, medical research, or service provision—where open source content sharing is not a norm, rules of the road for governing networks and networked organizations may need to be invented.

The reconfiguration of business forms and the development of hybrid governance models will undoubtedly stress the laws, regulations, and cultures that have developed in isolated silos. We will not only see the blending of market and nonmarket organizations, we will see the corresponding development of new approaches to funding, finance, and reporting requirements.

....

[36] Kanter, Beth, "Twestival: Here Comes Everyone to Raise Money for charity: water." *BlogHer*, January 25, 2009. Retrieved from http://www.blogher.com/twestival-here-comes-everyone-raise-money-twitter-charity-water.

[37] Allan, Nicole, "The Netroots Effect." *The Atlantic*, September 2009. Retrieved from http://www.theatlantic.com/doc/200909u/netroots.

Creating new modes of governance will be an important endeavor in the future, but in the near term it poses quite a challenge to the relationships between capital providers and social sector institutions. Will foundations find ways to fund dispersed, fluid, unincorporated organizations like Ushahidi and Nonprofitmapping.org? And if not, will they fail to be a consequential source of capital for these organizations? Will new organizational forms necessitate the overhaul of nonprofit tax and regulatory law? Will governments need to review and revise the very definition of nonprofit status?

MORE AND BETTER DATA, MORE READILY AVAILABLE AND AT LOWER COST

Here the public sector is leading the way. Governments at the municipal (San Francisco,[38] Washington, D.C.[39]), state,[40] and federal (data.gov, the Open Government Initiative) levels are making data available on the web. In the arena of campaign finance, the Sunlight Foundation enables users to tease out who gives how much money to whom, when they give it, and (by implication) why. On the Pew Charitable Trusts' Subsidyscope website, users can track federal subsidies.

As more such data become available, new correlations and connections will be revealed in every area in which philanthropy has an interest, from test scores of middle-schoolers to disparities in public health to racial discrimination in housing. The ability to mix and remix public data will influence both governmental and philanthropic approaches to producing social good.[41]

Of course, most government data are not accessible via the web. And philanthropy (with some important exceptions) has been even less pro-active in making data available. It's not yet known what force—third-party intermediaries, regulation, the market, leadership

---

[38] http://datasf.org/.

[39] http://data.octo.dc.gov/.

[40] "Stimulus and the States," Stateline.org. Retrieved from http://www.stateline.org/live/static/The_Stimulus_and_the_States.

[41] Paul Hawken, in his book *Blessed Unrest*, discusses systems change possibilities from this viewpoint, focusing on nonprofit organizations with similar missions.

within the field—will drive an opening-up of philanthropy, but open access to philanthropically funded data and research is within our reach. To the degree that new data will lead to new measurements of change, we should also expect to see major changes in the sector.[42]

A relatively recent innovation is the storage of information in "the cloud." The cloud refers to data and applications that are hosted remotely (i.e., stored on third-party servers) and that can be accessed via the web. The best-known examples are probably Facebook, Google Mail and Google Docs, Flickr, and SalesForce.com. Shifting from data storage on desktops or mainframes to cloud computing can save organizations money on hardware and software and allow them to allocate human resources differently.

BEYOND THE HORIZON

We can't predict what philanthropy will look like in five years, let alone ten. But it's safe to say that information networks will continue to proliferate, become more efficient, and become more accessible to more people and organizations. So too will new organizational forms, enabled by networks, informed by data, and motivated by the values of sharing and open participation, continue to proliferate. If foundations remain mainly top-down, centralized, reactive institutions while most of the innovation in philanthropy occurs along the long tail of funders and nonprofits, will the traditional power dynamic between donors and doers still obtain?

The resurgence of interest in the commons, as exemplified by the over 140,000 photos currently under Creative Commons license on Flickr, is perhaps a harbinger of things to come. Just as agrarian communities managed pasture land for the good of the whole and didn't inevitably suffer from the "tragedy of the commons," efforts such

---

[42] Steven Johnson, *The Invention of Air: A Story of Science, Faith, Revolution and the Birth of America.* New York: Riverhead Books, 2008, p. 69.

as the Public Library of Science, not to mention Wikipedia, show how information resources can be managed for the good of the whole.[43]

How will quasi-market entities such as B Corps and L3Cs evolve, and what new hybrids are yet to emerge? What changes might regulatory structures such as intellectual property law or patent regulation bring to bear on these emergent forms? What challenges might hybrids raise to the legal systems that define and shape charitable activity, such as nonprofit tax exemption or nonprofit status itself? Each of these questions has taken on much greater salience in the last couple of years and all will put pressure on federal and state governments to look at the sector differently.

While industry and the public sector, especially the Department of Defense, have for years used simulation technology and game-playing pedagogy to test new ideas and teach new skills, philanthropic support for games is newer and less well established. One significant example of where games have worked is in HopeLab's development of Re-Mission, a video game for youth living with cancer that helps them stick to their medicine regimens. Independent evaluations found a significant increase of regimen adherence by young people who played the game. Organizations such as Games for Change and the Serious Games Initiative are helping build awareness of these "pro-social" games. Games and mobile phones—in fact all digital technologies—readily lend themselves to quantitative measurement.

> Some of the areas that philanthropy concerns itself with are more likely to see significant benefit from a highly networked nonprofit sector than are others.

The decentralizing effects of networked technologies are now familiar. But there is also a counter-tendency: the creation of seemingly

---

[43] David Bollier and Lawrence Lessig are two of the foremost thinkers on the power of the commons in the digital age. Bollier's book *Viral Spiral: How the Commoners Built a Digital Republic of Their Own* traces the history and transition of commons law from the Internet to other areas of society.

"natural" monopolies on the web. Through a certain ineluctable logic—sellers want to go where the most buyers are, and buyers want to go where the most sellers are—the online auction business has produced a single major player, eBay. Similar logic has produced, at times shockingly quickly, natural monopolies among online payment systems (PayPal), classified ad hosting (Craigslist), user-generated video hosting (YouTube), and social networking sites (Facebook, which appears to be in the process of dethroning MySpace). Among all the many online giving markets, will the logic of monopoly formation—donors want to go where the most doers are, and doers want to go where the most donors are—produce a single dominant site with a single methodology of operation and assessment? If a monopoly does emerge, what are the implications?

How will better data sharing affect the way individuals donate? Will people be more aware of social problems and donate more, growing the philanthropic pie? Will "issue fatigue" set in, causing them to donate less? Will the plethora of competing sites, networks, ratings systems, and the like lead to data, and analytic, overload? This is a time of great entrepreneurial activity, and claims of the "new, new thing" are coming fast and furious. Lately we've begun to see some mergers and collaborations among networking ventures, but such cooperation may not become a trend and may not be healthy for the sector if it does.

Will more and better data raise awareness of "root cause" problems, as with the "scientific philanthropy" of a century ago, resulting in a redistribution of individual small donations—away from, say, the local church and toward organizations engaged with widespread social issues? Will donations become less focused on the local and more toward the regional, national, or international? To date we have no metrics to analyze these phenomena.

Will a generational split emerge? That is, will older people, who are less wired, remain attached to the old ways, while younger people give fewer dollars to the Salvation Army and United Way and more dollars to Kiva and DonorsChoose? Such a generational pattern seems already to be emerging in faith-based philanthropy, particularly among Jews and Catholics. Will there be a similar class-based split, reflective of the so-called digital divide? Are alternative giving approaches "good" for philanthropy, or will they effectively slice and dice donations into smaller, and less effective, pieces?

How will networked technologies affect the major volunteer civil society organizations—Rotary, Kiwanis, Big Brothers Big Sisters, Habitat for Humanity, and others? How will they affect donations to religious groups? These are the vehicles through which most Americans donate their time and money, and they represent, in the aggregate, a much larger segment of the philanthropic sector than do the staffed foundations. What will it mean for these organizations if younger, better-off individuals begin to gravitate in significant numbers away from them and toward DonorsChoose or Kiva? What will older organizations do with technology to stay current or even ahead of the curve?

In an analysis of the financial models of American theatre, opera, orchestra, and dance companies, William Baumol and William Bowen identified "cost disease" as the fundamental financing problem that bedevils arts organizations.[44] In most sectors of the economy, Baumol and Bowen noted, technology tends to increase productivity. There are, however, certain labor-intensive activities, such as an orchestra's producing live symphonic music, that undergo little or no growth in productivity through better technology over time. Relative to the rest of the economy, these activities become ever more expensive: they suffer from cost disease.

Likewise, some of the areas that philanthropy concerns itself with are more likely to see significant benefit from a highly networked nonprofit sector than are others. For example, improved networking will almost certainly make vaccination research more efficient. But what of a labor-intensive human service like foster care? Technology may improve foster child placement service around the edges, by

---

[44] Baumol, William J., and William G. Bowen, *Performing Arts: The Economic Dilemma.* New York: Twentieth Century Fund, 1966.

streamlining management and financial tasks, but at the most basic level, foster care consists of one family agreeing to take in one child, multiplied many times over. Though networking may spread the acceptance of best practices more quickly, there's only so much efficiency new technologies can bring to this arrangement. The same is true for homeless shelters, soup kitchens, and mentoring programs for troubled students. Labor-intensive endeavors like these can't be made very much more efficient; relative to medical research, human services will become more costly over time. Will the program areas that benefit most from new technologies become more attractive to philanthropy? Will the least technologically efficient and most costly subsectors see their government funding reduced?

Finally, how will the legal and institutional structures of philanthropy keep pace with the new modes of organizing, facilitating, informing, and funding change that technology facilitates? What new forms of accountability will emerge? How will institutional funders work with distributed networks? What new policy frames are necessary to maximize the potential impact of these new social forms and minimize their downsides? What new governance structures may emerge?

Conclusion

Philanthropy in the United States is entering a new phase. Through many independent actions we are building an information infrastructure that will connect the long tail of donors to the long tail of doers. This infrastructure has the potential to open up and systematize processes and decision-making practices that have heretofore occurred exclusively behind closed doors.

The outline of philanthropy's future is visible in online, shared portfolios of loans, as well as in informal networks of volunteers working together to aid disaster relief workers. It's visible in commercial firms seeking social missions and in the capital they attract to the sector. It's visible in policy debates about nonprofit tax privileges, in shared platforms for measures of social return, and in peer networks of individual donors. It's visible in foundation-led explorations of networked governance models and in community-based experiments with local fundraisers networked across time zones. We can see the outline of philanthropy's future in shared databases of scientific research, in real-time sharing of grants data in exportable, mashable data streams, and in small teams of app developers who find practical and unexpected uses for these data.

How are these phenomena shaping how donors give and how doers get things done? The forms that will animate philanthropy ten years from now don't yet exist. In the meantime, we can agree not to fear, scorn, or ignore new technologies but to be open to learning about them, experimenting with them, and sharing the results. We can reconsider assumptions built into our work over decades—assumptions that may no longer make sense, such as whether to fund informal networks, how individual entrepreneurs fit in the ecosystem of the social sector, and what kinds of copyrights (if any) advance the social missions we are pursuing. We can share ideas and data from the online marketplaces of individual givers with the large professionally staffed foundations, and vice versa. There are innumerable strategic and tactical approaches for us—as philanthropic institutions, as social-purpose organizations, and as individual donors—to consider in this moment of transition.

It is a scary time for many, a time of unprecedented opportunity for others. Just a few years ago we could not have imagined using dispersed networks of cell phones to report on earthquake damage and relief operations. Doing so seems obvious now. We cannot foresee what the next application of technology to improving social conditions will be—we can only be sure that it will seem obvious in retrospect. Meanwhile, what we can do is facilitate the behaviors and expectations of sharing structured data that will make that application possible.

We cannot assume that the inequities of access and capacity that still prevent so many individuals and institutions from using these new tools of change will disappear on their own. We must work to set policies and programs that will ensure connectivity for all. We must grasp the authentic beginnings of what information networks have enabled, and be prepared for faster, smarter, farther-reaching, and more innovative opportunities—for a philanthropy that's truly effective.

Resources

Baumol, William J., and William G. Bowen, *Performing Arts: The Economic Dilemma*. New York: Twentieth Century Fund, 1966.

Benkler, Yochai, *The Wealth of Networks: How Social Production Transforms Markets and Freedom*. New Haven: Yale University Press, 2006.

Bollier, David, *Viral Spiral: How the Commoners Built a Digital Republic of Their Own*. London: The New Press, 2008.

Doctorow, Cory, *Content: Selected Essays on Technology, Creativity, Copyright and the Future of the Future*. San Francisco: Tachyon Publications, 2008.

Fine, Allison, *Momentum: Igniting Social Change in the Connected Age*. San Francisco: Jossey-Bass, 2006.

Hawken, Paul, *Blessed Unrest: How the Largest Movement in the World Came into Being and Why No One Saw It Coming*. New York: Viking Press, 2007.

Hess, Charlotte, and Elinor Ostrom (eds), *Understanding Knowledge as a Commons: From Theory to Practice*. Cambridge, MA: MIT Press, 2007.

Johnson, Steven, *The Invention of Air: A Story of Science, Faith, Revolution and the Birth of America*. New York: Riverhead Books, 2008.

Kot, Greg, *Ripped: How the Wired Generation Revolutionized Music*. New York: Scribner & Sons, 2009.

Lessig, Lawrence, *Remix: Making Art and Culture Thrive in the Hybrid Economy*. London: Penguin Press, 2008.

Li, Charlene, and Josh Bernoff, *Groundswell: Winning in a World Transformed by Social Technologies*. Cambridge, MA: Harvard Business School Press, 2008.

Moulitsas Zuniga, Markos, *Taking on the System: Rules for Radical Change in a Digital Era*. New York: Penguin Books, 2008.

Shirky, Clay, *Here Comes Everybody: The Power of Organizing Without Organizations*. London: Penguin Press, 2008.

Sunstein, Cass R, *Infotopia: How Many Minds Produce Knowledge*. Oxford, U.K.: Oxford University Press, 2006.

Watson, Tom, *Causewired: Plugging in, Getting Involved, Changing the World*. New York: John C. Wiley, 2008.

Zittrain, Jonathan, *The Future of the Internet and How to Stop It*. New Haven: Yale University Press, 2008.

BLOGGERS

Lucy Bernholz: http://philanthropy.blogspot.com/
Allison Fine: http://afine2.wordpress.com/
The Intrepid Philanthropist: http://cspcs.sanford.duke.edu/blog
Beth Kanter: http://beth.typepad.com/
Tom Watson: http://tomwatson.typepad.com/

OTHER WEBSITES

http://www.moderngiving.com/
http://www.netsquared.org/
http://nten.org/
http://networkweaver.blogspot.com/
http://www.workingwikily.com/

Made in the USA
San Bernardino, CA
19 June 2013